Horns, Claws and Jaws

By M.W. Gough

There are no dinosaurs now, but they left fossils.

Fossils are prints of bones left in rocks.

Fossils have taught us lots about dinosaurs.

We once thought all dinosaurs had scales.

Then we saw fossils
with feather prints!

Dinosaurs didn't just walk about.
Some could fly!

Here's a dinosaur that was the size of a hawk.
It crawled up trees
and then launched itself off
to fly.

This dinosaur was very tall. It sought leaves and stalks from the treetops.

This dinosaur didn't withdraw from fights!

If it got into a fight,
it fought back with its horns.

This dinosaur caught its prey with sharp claws.

This dinosaur had strong jaws.

It stalked its prey
and then caught the prey
in its jaws!

Dinosaurs sought safe spots to pause and lay eggs.

But other dinosaurs might haul the eggs off to eat!

What might it be like
if dinosaurs still walked
across the land?

You ought to pause
and give it some thought!

CHECKING FOR MEANING

1. What are fossils? *(Literal)*
2. How did dinosaurs with strong jaws catch their prey? *(Literal)*
3. How do we know some dinosaurs could fly? *(Inferential)*

EXTENDING VOCABULARY

sought	What is the base word of *sought*? What is another word or words the author could have used instead of *sought*?
stalk	The words *stalks* and *stalked* are used in this text. *Stalks* is a noun and *stalked* is a verb. What are the two meanings of the base word *stalk*?
haul	What does the word *haul* mean? What is another word the author could have used instead of *haul*?

MOVING BEYOND THE TEXT

1. Where might you see dinosaur fossils on display? Have you ever seen a dinosaur fossil? Was it a dinosaur with horns, claws or jaws?

2. What did you already know about dinosaurs before reading this book? What do you still want to learn?

3. Why is it important to study fossils and other things from the past? What can people learn from these studies?

4. The dinosaurs in this book used their horns, claws and jaws to eat and defend themselves. What other animals have special body parts? How do those animals use their special body parts?

TIME TO WRITE

Write about what the world would be like if dinosaurs were still around. How might their horns, claws and jaws cause trouble for people?

PRACTICE WORDS